Ancestral Rites

of Passage

Journal

Emme Rain

Cover design by Jesse Kimmel-Freeman
Cover Photo by Jeremy Bishop on Unsplash
Book design by Jesse Kimmel-Freeman

http://www.lanicomediahouse.com/

If you are unable to order this book from your local bookseller, you may order directly from the publisher.

ISBN: 978-0-9986520-4-7
10 9 8 7 6 5 4 3 2 1
Printed in the United States of America.

I honor my ancestors for the work I was able to share in this book. My mom, Dorothy Pugh and grandmother, Annie Hardaway as well as all the other highly honored ones that went before me. I dedicate this book to my children and grandchildren, those who one day will call me an ancestor. This is what legacy is all about, the passing on of greatness, inspiration, and assets. May all the readers come to appreciate what was passed down through their family lineage and discover the hidden gems. Ase!

A Word About Bloodline Trauma and Family Dysfunction

In the years that I've been doing ancestral work, I've come to appreciate the difficulty in desiring a connection with ancestors when you come from a dysfunctional family or have a tragic history with those ancestors you remember. It can be difficult to see the wisdom or power in connecting with the energy of people who blew their life on gambling, drugging, drinking, and other forms of debauchery. And if you were physically, sexually or verbally abused, then it can seem like a slap in the face to be asked to reconnect with those energies again.

First, remember this is YOUR journey and you are never going to be forced to do anything you don't want to do. You can begin slowly with the energies you are most comfortable with. If and when you feel strong enough, or ready, you can then move into healing those traumas and tragedies. You don't have to attempt to fix it all at one time. Take it a step at a time, a small bite at a time. Above all, remember you are the one who lives, breathes, the walking ambassador of the bloodline. You are not a victim any longer. You are approaching this as the healer with authority to move on behalf of the whole bloodline.

Also, there is a powerful benefit to healing traumas. The chief of them all is the freedom and power you pass on to your children and the children of others in your family line. Can you imagine living a life that didn't start with the drama you saw? Can you imagine how much freer and farther along you would be without the tragedies? This is the gift you'd be passing on. If anything motivates me to stay the course, it is the face of my children and grandchildren. There are some experiences I never wish for them to have. I want to see them free of the burden of twisted knowledge and too much responsibility too early on. Thus, I work on the predominant energy of the family so that they drink from a cleaner cup and drink in a sense of support and empowerment.

Lastly, I never recommend quitting, but taking a break is necessary sometimes. If you feel overwhelmed, honor yourself and give yourself permission to step back, defrag and come back at it later from a healthy space. Your healing work should not break your sanity or ruin your lifestyle. It should add to and enhance it all. That's not to say that healing doesn't fracture things within us. It often breaks things that do not belong to us. And as we purge, it's okay to have a moment of silence and grief for the old parts we need to say goodbye to. In this way, you keep coming back stronger and stronger, not broken, weary or worn out. Take it at a pace that keeps you grounded. You will be doing this for a lifetime. No need to rush. This is a journey, not a destination.

With all my love and support,

Emme Rain

You are the culmination of everything that came before you. There is greatness within your lineage. Tap into it.

—Emme Rain

The *Ancestral Rites of Passage* is a 22-day process designed to assist you with going through spiritual initiations guided by the ancestors. This program is designed to remove ancestral bondage and infuse more energy into the bloodline.

What to expect?

The activities and journaling prompts in this workbook help activate and utilize beneficial aspects of yourself and your ancestors.

There will be a lot of healing and looking at self, but once activated, you and future generations will be able to tap into the skills and power needed for the continued elevation of your bloodline much easier.

Everyone that completes this process successfully will experience a whole new level of power, joy, healing, and happiness in their life.

Make space for the process.

This 22-day process is designed to help you build a stronger connection with your ancestors and call forth their most empowered assistance. Dedicate at least one hour each day to completing the exercises and writing prompts in this journal.

Tools you will need to support the process:
- White candles (jar, pillars, votives, tea lights etc.)
- White Roses
- Magickal Mystic oils or candles - Family Restoration, Bloodline Cleanse, Open Roads, Ancestors
- Any other oils and herbs of your choosing

Clarity is Key

Day One

What would you like to improve, call forth, or activate in your life?

Would you like to see the restoration of your family, better health, new skills, and more talents? Write them all down. Prioritize what you feel you need more in this moment.

_____

_____

_____

_____

_____

_____

_____

_____

_____

Day One ─◦ Continued◦─

Day Two

By understanding epigenetics, you can shift the way your body reads your DNA, tap into, and activate the best traits and aspects of your bloodline and change the trajectory of your lineage from this point forward.

Think of traits that could make your life easier, your relationships better and that can secure your health and wealth. Write a list of traits. For example, would being more creative make it easier for you to identify new opportunities or express your strengths?

Don't worry about whether you know family members who have these traits. Simply write down all the traits. Next to each trait, write out how it can serve and strengthen you within your personal life and your entire bloodline.

Day Two — *Continued*

This list should fill the page. You're going to have to put some thought into it. The more you think about what you want and how it will benefit you, the easier it becomes to manifest and create.

Here are some examples of traits:

1. Wisdom
2. Patience
3 Business acumen
4. Charm and wit
5. Strategy
6. Foresight
7. Boldness
8. Discipline

Day Two ⟶ Continued

Day Two →Continued←

Day Three

There are two types of ancestry. Physical ancestry includes all your descendants. Spiritual ancestry includes all the non-earthbound beings and origins that contributed to the creation of your soul. This includes gods, goddesses, and beings from other star systems.

For the purposes of this process, we will focus on the ancestry of the bloodline and what it represents.

For many, physical ancestry represents:
- History and Background
- Legacy Potentialities
- Immortality
- Interconnectivity

Day Three →Continued←

Reflect on what these things mean to you.

Your ancestors have timeless wisdom and more foresight than you can imagine. They also understand all aspects of the human condition. Many of them are vested in the well-being and the success of your bloodline.

How would you like your connection with your ancestors to help you change the trajectory of your lineage?

_____

_____

_____

_____

_____

_____

_____

Day Three ⇀Continued⇀

Day Three ⇒ Continued⇐

Day Three ~Continued~

Now that you know your ancestors are vested in your well-being and success, what changes are you willing to make in your daily life to create time and space to connect with them more?

_____

_____

_____

_____

_____

_____

_____

_____

_____

_____

_____

Day Three ➤Continued◄

_____

_____

_____

_____

_____

_____

_____

_____

_____

_____

_____

_____

_____

_____

_____

_____

_____

_____

_____

_____

_____

_____

_____

Call Forth Energy and Power

Day Four

Going through the ancestral rites of passage is an alchemical process. To fulfill your role as ambassador to your bloodline, it will be necessary to transmute all the active undesirable traits within your DNA.

Today, sit in nature 30 minutes and call forth the residual energy of your ancestors left here on Earth. Call for it to come to you clean, pure, ready to use for the elevation of the entire bloodline.

After you call forth the residual energy of your ancestors pay attention to feelings, thoughts, senses, and surroundings.

Day Four ~Continued~

What body sensations, thoughts, feelings came up for you during the day after completing the exercise?

_____

_____

_____

_____

_____

_____

_____

_____

_____

_____

_____

_____

_____

_____

Day Four ⇝Continued⇜

_____

_____

_____

_____

_____

_____

_____

_____

_____

_____

_____

_____

_____

_____

_____

_____

Day Five

Ask your ancestors to harmoniously assist in removing all obstacles of communication between you and them. Also ask them to help open the door of complete unity within your bloodline under your ambassadorship. Tell them that you are willing to fully tap into the knowledge and power of your bloodline today and everyday

Use a Bloodline Cleanse or Open Roads candle and/or oil to support your prayer if you have it. The candles and oils mentioned here can be found at MagickalMystic.com. Otherwise, dress a tall white candle with the oils and herbs you have available. Let it burn straight through if possible.

Please always practice fire safety.

Day Five →Continued←

Each day that your candle is burning, journal
any dreams, ideas, or messages you receive.

_____

_____

_____

_____

_____

_____

_____

_____

_____

_____

_____

_____

_____

Day Five ➛ Continued ←

_____

_____

_____

_____

_____

_____

_____

_____

_____

_____

_____

_____

_____

_____

_____

_____

Day Five →Continued←

_____

_____

_____

_____

_____

_____

_____

_____

_____

_____

_____

_____

_____

_____

_____

_____

_____

Day Six

One day you will take your place among the ancestors. The future generations of your bloodline will need the strengths and skill-sets you possess. So, everything you are doing now is of the utmost importance. Whatever is in your lineage that you fail to address will continue beyond you. Take time to ensure you are satisfied with the aspects of your bloodline that you are currently activating. Do you want these aspects to continue, or do you need further adjustments?

Take a moment to imagine and feel the energy of Jupiter which is expansion. Call forth this expansion of all that you desire for your bloodline and freedom from everything that has held your bloodline back from expressing its greatness and abundance. Imagine Jupiter's expansive energy infusing into your bloodline and DNA.

Day Six → *Continued*

Visualize your bloodline being expanded in every area that you feel needs expansion. Also, visualize that energy being projected into future generations.

Write down how you felt during this exercise. Write down any ideas or inspirations that come to you after completing this exercise.

_____

_____

_____

_____

_____

_____

_____

_____

_____

Day Six ⇝Continued⇜

_____

_____

_____

_____

_____

_____

_____

_____

_____

_____

_____

_____

_____

_____

_____

_____

_____

Day Six ➤ Continued

_____

_____

_____

_____

_____

_____

_____

_____

_____

_____

_____

_____

_____

_____

_____

_____

Day Seven

Pour libations for your entire bloodline past, present, and future. Pour libations into the earth or in a live plant.

Sit still and imagine all your ancestors being present with you and your candle as it burns. While sitting, journal what ideas, thoughts, wisdom, and inspirations come to you.

_____

_____

_____

_____

_____

_____

_____

_____

_____

Day Seven ⇢Continued⇠

_____

_____

_____

_____

_____

_____

_____

_____

_____

_____

_____

_____

_____

_____

_____

_____

Day Seven ~Continued~

_____

_____

_____

_____

_____

_____

_____

_____

_____

_____

_____

_____

_____

_____

_____

_____

Choose

Love,

Unification,

and

Greatness

Day Eight

Many people have ancestors or family patterns that they are not proud of. Having anger and resentment towards ancestors is dangerous. Division and separation based upon what you know of your ancestors is dangerous. Feeling undeserving of full cooperation of your ancestors is also dangerous. Therefore, you must expand your mind and heart. Love ALL of what is within you and your ancestors. Love and accept the good, the bad, the ugly, the unknown, and the known.

Choose love and unification from this point forward. With a sure direction in mind and heart, you get all the best of whatexists in your bloodline.

Day Eight — Continued

Use a white candle, white roses, and Family Restoration candle – if you have it. Pray and set the intention to LOVINGLY unify the entirety of yourself and your bloodline. You want to hold the candle to your heart until you feel loved and the feeling of unification. When you light it, see yourself as a single entity, empowered, a true ambassador, enlightened, and inspired to take action as you build your family legacy.

Day Eight → Continued←

Do you feel more unified with your ancestors and a sense of greatness? Do you feel more empowered to improve your life and your lineage? In what ways do you feel inspired to take action?

_____

_____

_____

_____

_____

_____

_____

_____

_____

_____

_____

_____

_____

_____

_____

Day Eight →Continued←

Day Eight → Continued←

Day Nine

Whether we address it or not, all of us have reservations in life concerning various things. Many times, we pair up with others who share our passions AND our reservations, so there is no resistance, no challenge, and no growth.

Today you must list what your reservations are. Are you leery of working with blood or speaking to the dead? Sit with yourself, discover the truth, and create your list.

There are some rites you will not be able to take, some paths you cannot walk, some things you cannot have, if you do not overcome your hang-ups and do not master your reservations.

Day Nine ~Continued~

By first knowing your reservations you can decide what you can work through and what you can work around.

What are your reservations?

_____

_____

_____

_____

_____

_____

_____

_____

_____

_____

_____

_____

_____

Day Nine ➤Continued➤

_____

_____

_____

_____

_____

_____

_____

_____

_____

_____

_____

_____

_____

_____

_____

_____

_____

_____

Day Nine ~Continued~

_____

_____

_____

_____

_____

_____

_____

_____

_____

_____

_____

_____

_____

_____

_____

Day Ten

No family is without shameful, painful, or inglorious aspects. The thing is to understand the source of bloodline fractures and fissures within your family and then begin offering up the sources of the issues. Things like poverty, broken self-esteem, and perversion. To release them, you must first rise above the emotional responses you've been having to them. For this to work you must be the healer, you cannot be the judge.

Day Ten ~Continued~

Prepare one of your white candles for healing and unity by adding a drop of your blood to the candle. Remember, healing energy is the energy of correction, restoration, fortification, and alignment. Think thoughts of wholeness and empowerment as you perform today's exercise.

If you ABSOLUTELY cannot use blood, you may use some of your hair. Pray and set the intention for the healing of shame, pain, sickness of every kind, poverty, jealousy, and any thing that you feel needs to be healed with you and your bloodline. Envision the healing complete and the unity strong and unshakeable. Sit with the candle for at least 30 minutes.

Day Ten →*Continued*←

What feelings and thoughts come up as you sit with the candle? Do you feel that you have addressed all that needs to be healed in your bloodline?

_____

_____

_____

_____

_____

_____

_____

_____

_____

_____

_____

_____

_____

_____

Day Ten ➤ Continued

_____

_____

_____

_____

_____

_____

_____

_____

_____

_____

_____

_____

_____

_____

_____

_____

Day Ten ⇒Continued⇐

_____

_____

_____

_____

_____

_____

_____

_____

_____

_____

_____

_____

_____

_____

_____

_____

_____

_____

Enter

the

Gates

Day Eleven

FIRST RITES (GATE OF ILLUMINATION)
SACRED WORDS OF POWER:
AH FAS AH POL EH DOS VEH HA SOL
That is pronounced like ahh, fahsss (long s), pole, eh, dos (like the Spanish word), veh, ha (emphasis on ha with a strong breath), sooooul

The gate of illumination is awareness and understanding. You are now conscious that you are not separate or better than anything that came before you and you now know that you have the power to change whatever you feel must be changed, and the power to amplify what you feel must be amplified.

If you have made it this far in the process, it is it time to use the Sacred Words of Power to perform your first rite of passage. These words are like a key to enter in through the gate of illumination. If you are ready your sleep patterns may change and entering the gate will feel warm and accepting.

$\mathcal{D}ay$ $\mathcal{E}leven$ →Continued←

If you are not ready, you will need to perform the rite again. You will be granted passage once you have cleared your heavy heart, anger, guilt, judgment, and any fractures in your soul.

Was your first rite a success? If so, what changes are you experiencing? If not, what still needs to be cleared in order for you to move forward?

_____

_____

_____

_____

_____

_____

_____

_____

_____

_____

_____

_____

Day Eleven →Continued←

Day Twelve

There are some subtle differences between what is available to you from your mother's lineage and what is available to you from your father's lineage. It is vital to learn to tell the difference in where messages are coming from.

In this exercise focus on the maternal side of your bloodline.

Today, think of a question you want answered from your maternal bloodline and write them down. Call them forth and ask them to commune with you all day. Pour some libations for them if you can. Light an incense. Rub your earlobes with Ancestor oils.

Day Twelve → *Continued*

Make note of how your body temperature feels, how your eyes feel, if you get certain tastes in your mouth, etc. Record any downloads, ideas, inspirations, feelings, sensations, dreams, or visions that you receive. Not just what was said or shown to you, but also the modality in which it was received.

What question did you ask and what information did you receive from your maternal bloodline?

_____

_____

_____

_____

_____

_____

_____

_____

_____

Day Twelve ➤ Continued

_____

_____

_____

_____

_____

_____

_____

_____

_____

_____

_____

_____

_____

_____

_____

_____

_____

Day Thirteen

In this exercise focus on the paternal side of your bloodline.

To prevent bleed-over and create an authentic experience, think of different questions you want answered from your paternal bloodline and write them down.

Call them forth and ask them to commune with you all day. Pour some libations for them if you can. Light an incense. Rub your earlobes with Ancestor oils.

Day Thirteen →Continued←

Make note of how your body temperature feels, how your eyes feel, if you get certain tastes in your mouth, etc. Record any downloads, ideas, inspirations, feelings, sensations, dreams, or visions that you receive. Not just what was said or shown to you, but also the modality in which it was received.

What question did you ask and what information did you receive from your paternal bloodline?

_____

_____

_____

_____

_____

_____

_____

_____

Day Thirteen →Continued←

Day Thirteen →Continued←

Day Fourteen

For many the inability to heal has been tied to the belief that they must remain righteously angry, when in reality release and separation may be the best course of action. If you have challenges with living family members you can release, purge, even punish without pain, bitterness and deep-seated anger becoming your reality. Lovingly release bloodline grudges, hatred, and anger, and open the path for an even deeper unification.

Day Fourteen ~Continued~

Get a sheet of paper and write out in great detail all the stuff you need to release from your heart and mind regarding living family members. Release sexual abuse, physical abuse, lies, mistreatment, and any other traumas you can remember. Burn a small white candle over it, pray to transmute the energy of all you wrote. Tonight, before bed, you can then take it outside and burn it and let the wind carry the ashes. Time to be free!

What thoughts and emotional responses did you experience as you burned and released all the things on your list?

_____

_____

_____

_____

_____

_____

Day Fourteen →Continued←

_____

_____

_____

_____

_____

_____

_____

_____

_____

_____

_____

_____

_____

_____

_____

_____

_____

Day Fifteen

Identify one thing that you cannot do for yourself or by yourself. Give your ancestors an assignment. Call forth the energies present within your bloodline that can assist with the task. For example, you can charge the healers in your bloodline with working on the areas of weakness in your physical body and acquiring the knowledge necessary to live in alignment with wholeness in order for you to experience a pain-free week.

Do not seek outside counsel about what you should activate. Begin to trust your own inner eye. This is an activation of specific aspects so that you can see what it feels like and looks like when you're actually successful at tapping into ancestral power.

Day Fifteen →Continued←

What was your request?

How did it feel to make a request to your ancestors?

_____

_____

_____

_____

_____

_____

_____

_____

_____

_____

_____

_____

_____

_____

_____

Day Fifteen →Continued←

_____

_____

_____

_____

_____

_____

_____

_____

_____

_____

_____

_____

_____

_____

_____

_____

Day Fifteen →Continued←

_____

_____

_____

_____

_____

_____

_____

_____

_____

_____

_____

_____

_____

_____

_____

_____

Day Sixteen

At this point you have connected with your maternal and paternal bloodline. You have also connected with all the mothers and fathers of both bloodlines. Next, you will need to call forth all the mothers from both the maternal and paternal sides. Welcome their love, nurturing, power, and support into your life.

Day Sixteen ~Continued~

Working with the mothers is extremely beneficial. You should keep the mothers strong to keep the power of the womb pure.

The mothers are also your go to for:

- Healing
- Wisdom and Direction
- Creation and Creativity, Other Chaos Magick
- Nurture and Revitalization
- Enchantments, Glamours
- Infusions and Expansions
- Love

To further enhance your connection with them give offerings to the mothers by burning a white candle for them and commit to at least 33 minutes of uninterrupted meditation where you envision yourself connecting with them.

Day Sixteen → *Continued*

Write down the inspirations, messages, sensations, feelings, dreams, and downloads you receive after reconnecting with the mothers.

_____

_____

_____

_____

_____

_____

_____

_____

_____

_____

_____

_____

_____

_____

_____

_____

_____

Day Sixteen → Continued

Day Seventeen

Working with the fathers of your paternal and maternal bloodline is as beneficial as working with the mothers, but in different ways.

Some of the benefits of energizing the fathers are:
- Protection
- Wisdom and Direction
- Order in all aspects of Life and Magick
- Restoration and Rejuvenation
- Creation and Enforcement of boundaries
- Ego and Body healing, also great for balancing emotions
- Inheritance

Day Seventeen →Continued←

To enhance your connection with them, give offerings to the fathers by burning a white candle for them and commit to at least 22 uninterrupted minutes of meditation where you envision yourself connecting with them.

Make it an event for them because there are many who may have never received the infusions of veneration from the living.

Write down the inspirations, messages, sensations, feelings, dreams, and downloads you receive after connecting with the fathers.

_____

_____

_____

_____

_____

Day Seventeen →Continued←

Day Seventeen →Continued←

_____

_____

_____

_____

_____

_____

_____

_____

_____

_____

_____

_____

_____

_____

_____

_____

_____

_____

Create
the
Shift

Day Eighteen

As your connection to your ancestors grows, keep in mind that the relationships are respectful partnerships. Your ancestors do not dictate what you do. They assist you in what you have already decided to do. There are dangers when you are in a state of obedience. The least of them being a repetition of the same life and thought patterns of those that came before you. You do not obey your ancestors or any other energy for that matter. You honor and you venerate. You do not worship. Bow to no one, no thing, and no energy.

You are the I AM. You are the final authority in your life. You are sovereign.

Day Eighteen ↠ Continued↞

Commit to being spiritually sovereign. Declare and affirm that you are fully sovereign. Embrace the fact that you are in control and have the final authority in all interactions and relationships.

Sovereignty is not something that can be claimed in half measures. It must be done fully, wholly, and completely.

What does sovereignty mean to you? How does it feel to declare your sovereignty?

_____

_____

_____

_____

_____

Day Eighteen →Continued←

_____

_____

_____

_____

_____

_____

_____

_____

_____

_____

_____

_____

_____

_____

_____

_____

_____

_____

Day Eighteen →Continued←

Day Nineteen

Within your cells there exists a perfect emotional recall of every detail of every life lived by your ancestral mothers and fathers. That means you have learned emotional responses and inherited emotional responses.

To release cellular trauma and rewrite the emotional aspects of any trauma you or your bloodline have experienced you will work with a white candle. Hold the candle to your heart and pray, declare and envision a harmonious release of all cellular trauma now. Light the candle then write a new narrative for the bloodline.

Traumas include but are not limited to abuse, slavery, rape, cheating, deception, rejection, abandonment, etc.

Day Nineteen →*Continued*←

Write the new narrative for your bloodline.

_____

_____

_____

_____

_____

_____

_____

_____

_____

_____

_____

_____

_____

_____

_____

_____

Day Nineteen →Continued←

Day Nineteen →Continued←

_____

_____

_____

_____

_____

_____

_____

_____

_____

_____

_____

_____

_____

_____

_____

_____

_____

_____

Day Twenty

The purpose of ancestral veneration is to:
- Amplify what is best within the bloodline
- Heal and rectify what is out of balance
- Strengthen your lineage
- Receive wisdom

Your cells hold the most perfect memory recall. Not only does the brain of the cell retain the memory of how the cell should function, but it also holds the emotional memories of your ancestors. That means during the process of calling forth what is most beneficial and releasing what is not you may experience the emotions that are attached to that trait.

Day Twenty →*Continued*←

It is your job to assign a new emotional story when necessary. Today sit in meditation and call forth your ancestors to sit with you. While you are sitting, create a new narrative around any non-beneficial emotional memories. Focus on turning all pain into power.

Write a new narrative for everything that has caused you pain.

_____

_____

_____

_____

_____

_____

_____

_____

Day Twenty → Continued

Day Twenty →Continued←

_____

_____

_____

_____

_____

_____

_____

_____

_____

_____

_____

_____

_____

_____

_____

_____

_____

_____

Day Twenty-One

The rites of passage are:
- Acceptance
- Unification
- Analysis
- Activation
- Authority

These rites of passage can change every aspect of your life and family. Some changes will be instant, and others will be gradual. Now that you have explored connecting and shifting you can continue to journal with confidence. For now, reflect on how this journey has been for you.

Day Twenty-One — Continued

Do you see a difference in your thought processes? Are you able to drop the emotions connected with old stories? How have your feelings been different? Have you felt more supported and connected?

_____

_____

_____

_____

_____

_____

_____

_____

_____

_____

_____

_____

_____

Day Twenty-One → Continued

Day Twenty-One →Continued←

_____

_____

_____

_____

_____

_____

_____

_____

_____

_____

_____

_____

_____

_____

_____

_____

_____

_____

_____

Day Twenty-Two

Twenty-two days is the length of this course, but this should be a life-long practice. You truly have the power to influence the trajectory of your bloodline. The exercises in this journal are not easy, but they are beneficial and empowering actions that you can do for yourself.

You will only reach greater levels of understanding the more you continue connecting with your ancestors. There is no right or wrong way to practice and you are now equipped to go far on this journey. You can tap into and work with forces that can move through time and space, and project energy that moves according to your will.

Day Twenty-Two → Continued←

Make a list of how you would like to unify and elevate your bloodline going forward.

_____

_____

_____

_____

_____

_____

_____

_____

_____

_____

_____

_____

_____

Day Twenty-Two → Continued←

Day Twenty-Two → Continued←

The Ancestral Rites of Passage is a 22-day process to connect you with your ancestors, so you can fortify and empower your lineage. Throughout this journey you will see shifts in your daily life and receive answers and guidance the moment you need it. Through thought-provoking writing prompts and healing exercises, you will learn how to access skills, talents, and abilities that are dormant within your bloodline and purge unbeneficial aspects. You will experience a healthier body and mind as well as abundance across all aspects of life, but only when you make this a lifestyle.

Emme Rain is an international best-selling author, keynote speaker, mentor, and business mogul. She has over 20 years of coaching and teaching experience in a variety of areas, including sexual and domestic violence, self-love, and healing, as well as personal and financial development. Her passion for personal development and teaching has led her to create Divinity Academy, a learning platform dedicated specifically to giving people the tools to become sovereign, abundant, and powerful.

Scan the QR code to connect with Emme Rain, shop from the Magickal Mystic website, or to learn more about the EmmePyre Emme Rain has created.

If you enjoyed this journal, please leave a review with the retailer you bought it from.

Made in the USA
Columbia, SC
31 March 2022